HARCOURT HORIZONS

Our State

HANDS-ON READING ACTIVITIES

Orlando   Austin   Chicago   New York   Toronto   London   San Diego

Visit *The Learning Site!*
www.harcourtschool.com

Dear Teacher,

We are proud to introduce you to *Harcourt Horizons Hands-On Reading Activities with the Bag Ladies*. We are the Bag Ladies, Karen Simmons and Cindy Guinn. We are teachers, working in the classroom every day just like YOU! It was our own love of teaching that led us into writing hands-on activities for other teachers to follow.

The activities in this book were especially designed to accompany each unit of the *Harcourt Horizons* social studies program. Combining Bag Ladies' activities with the *Harcourt Horizons* text motivates students and makes social studies "come alive." The projects can be done with students of any ability level and any language background. The blackline masters have few words, so those that do appear can be easily translated.

If you enjoy these activities and want to learn more about our Bag Ladies make-and-take workshops, educational materials, and upcoming events, you can go to *bagladiesonline.com* on the Internet. Visit *harcourtschool.com/socialstudies* for more social studies activities. HAVE FUN!

The Bag Ladies (Karen Simmons and Cindy Guinn)

Copyright © by Harcourt, Inc.

All rights reserved. No part of this publication may be reproduced or transmitted in any form or by any means, electronic or mechanical, including photocopy, recording, or any information storage and retrieval system, without permission in writing from the publisher.

Permission is hereby granted to individual teachers using the corresponding student's textbook or kit as the major vehicle for regular classroom instruction to photocopy Copying Masters from this publication in classroom quantities for instructional use and not for resale. Requests for information on other matters regarding duplication of this work should be addressed to School Permissions and Copyrights, Harcourt, Inc., 6277 Sea Harbor Drive, Orlando, Florida 32887-6777. Fax: 407-345-2418.

HARCOURT and the Harcourt Logo are trademarks of Harcourt, Inc., registered in the United States of America and/or other jurisdictions.

Printed in the United States of America

ISBN 0-15-336916-7

1 2 3 4 5 6 7 8 9 10 082 10 09 08 07 06 05 04 03

Contents

Our State Travel Bag 4

Unit 1–CD Case State Booklet 6

Unit 2–Envelope History Book 8

Unit 3–Step Through My State 10

Unit 4–Snap-Shut Bag Book 12

Unit 5–Design a Fact Hat 14

Unit 6–Fact Finder 16

Blackline Masters

Unit 1 Pattern 18

Unit 4 Pattern 19

Our State Travel Bag

Materials:
*Scissors
*Brown paper grocery bag
*Hole punch
*4 brass fasteners
*Craft foam
*Thin twine (4-6 inches)
*Black or brown tempera paint (optional)

Social Studies Skills:
*Geography
*Products
*Landmarks

Reading Skills:
*Main Idea
*Fact and Opinion
*Predicting

Instructions:
1. Lay out the bag with the flap at the bottom.

2. Fold down the top of the bag to about 1 inch above the bottom flap.

3. Open to the original position.

4. Cut away to the fold line all but the back layer. Save the cut-off part.

Illustrations:

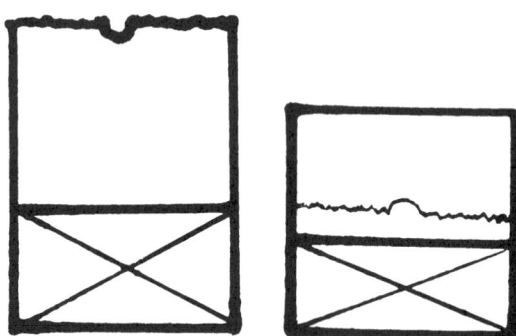

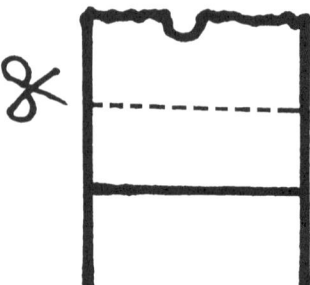

Hands-On Reading Activities

5. Round the edges of the flap to form the closure of the travel bag.

6. Open out the scrap that was cut from the bag, and fold the two ends to the middle. Fold one long side up to the middle and the other down over it. This will make the handle of the bag.

7. Punch a hole in each end of the handle. Push a brass fastener through each hole, and attach the handle to the top of the bag on the fold. Attach it about 1 inch in from each side so it will be rounded and easy to grasp.

8. Cut two shapes of fun foam and use brass fasteners to attach one to the flap of the bag and the other to the bag itself. Tie the piece of twine around the top piece of foam. Wrap it around the bottom piece to close the bag.

9. For a luggage look, crinkle the bag and then paint it with black or brown watered-down tempera paint.

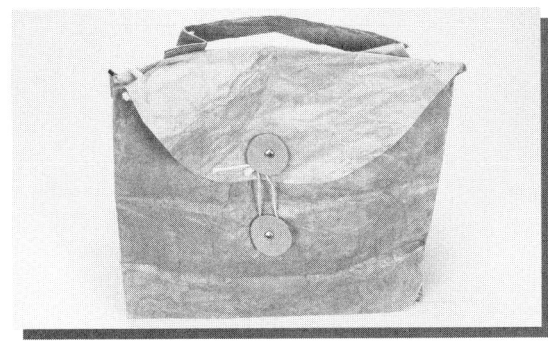

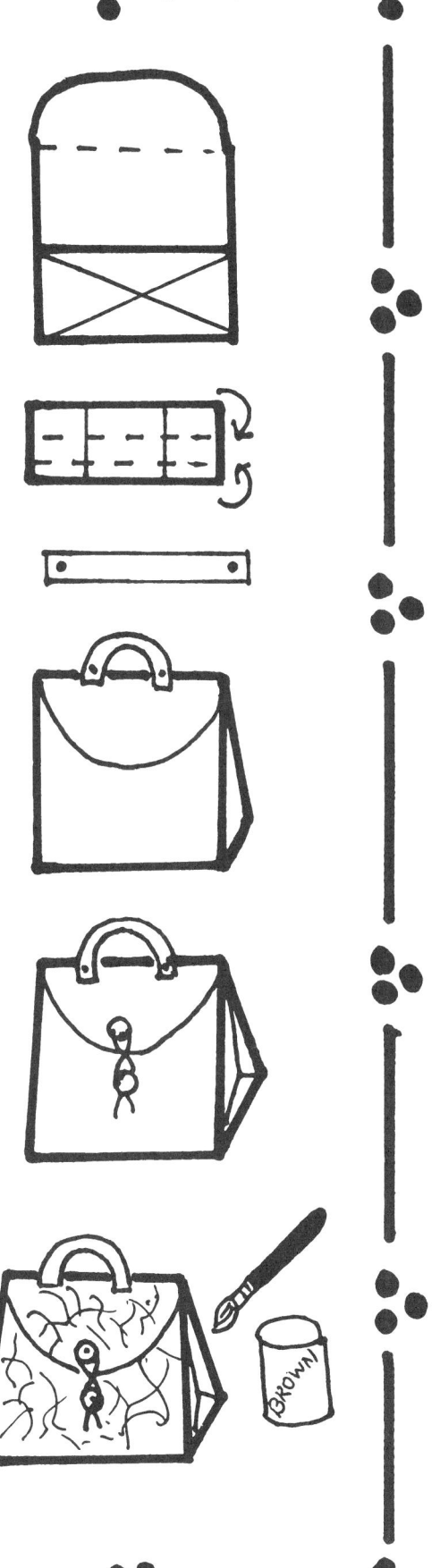

Hands-On Reading Activities

CD Case
State Booklet
Unit 1

Materials:

*Empty CD case
*Blackline master
*Colored pencils, markers, crayons
*Stapler

Social Studies Skills:

*Geography
*Climate
*Waterways

Reading Skills:

*Compound Words
*Summarizing
*Unfamiliar Words

Instructions:

1. Remove the cardboard insert from the CD case.

2. Make a CD case cover, and label it with your state and state slogan.

3. Make multiple copies of the CD blackline and staple them inside your CD cover.

Illustrations:

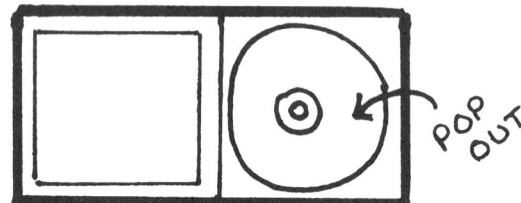

4. On the pages of the booklet, list important information from Unit 1, including landforms, rivers, natural regions, and climate.

5. Illustrate and label state plants and wildlife.

6. Add information about economic, population, and political regions.

Hands-On Reading Activities

Envelope History Book
Unit 2

Materials:

*Envelopes (any size or color but all the same)
*Scissors
*Crayons, markers, or colored pencils

Social Studies Skills:

*Early People
*State History
*Landmarks

Reading Skills:

*Compare/Contrast
*Generalize
*Cause/Effect

Instructions:

1. Choose one envelope to be your cover. Seal only this envelope.

2. Leave the left vertical edge of the cover envelope closed. Cut off the other three edges.

3. Cut a notch about 1 inch long at the top and bottom of the closed edge.

4. In the remaining envelopes, cut a 3- to 4-inch slit near the left vertical edge, leaving a 1/2-inch space above and below it.

Illustrations:

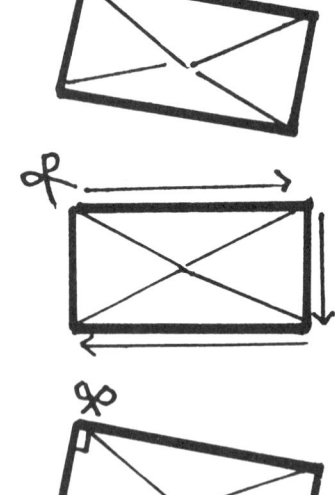

8

Hands-On Reading Activities

5. Stack all the slit envelopes, matching up the slits. The flaps of all the envelopes should be face down.

6. Open out the cover envelope and fold it the long way so that the notches are in the middle. (Do not crease.)

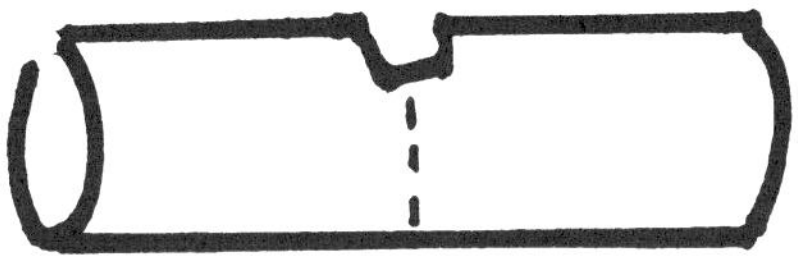

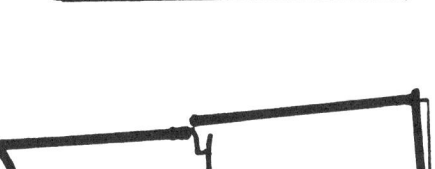

7. Slide the cover through the slits in the stacked envelopes, up to the notch. Then open the cover.

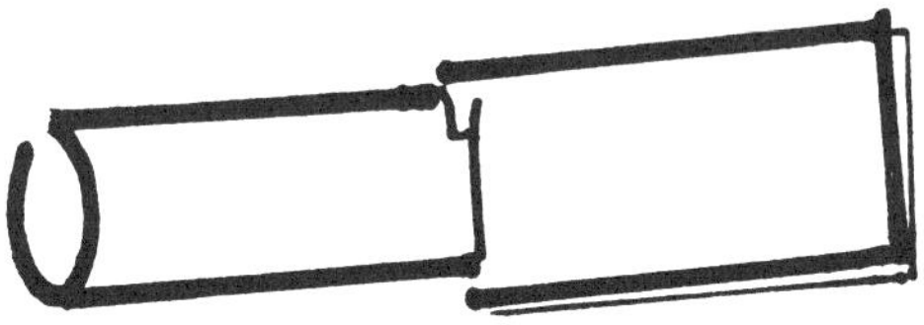

8. Title the book and decorate the cover. Label the envelopes with the topics covered in the unit. (Suggestions: Important people in state history, Early people, Early towns, etc.) Put into envelopes items that have to do with these topics.

Hands-On Reading Activities

9

Step Through My State
Unit 3

Materials:
*Three 11x17-inch sheets of paper
*Stapler
*Scissors
*Markers, colored pencils, crayons

Social Studies Skills:
*Settlers
*Conflict
*State Heroes

Reading Skills:
*Sequence
*Cause and Effect
*Unfamiliar Words

Instructions:
1. Stack the three sheets of paper so that the bottom of each page is 1 inch up from the bottom of the page below it.

2. Fold the top forward so that you see six levels of paper. Staple at the fold.

Illustrations:

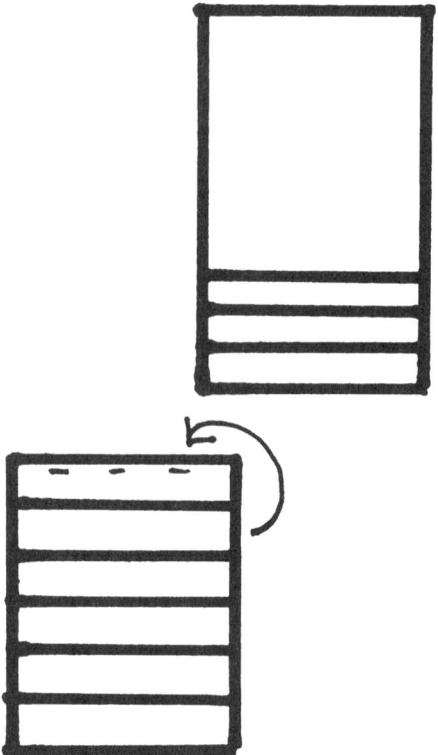

Hands-On Reading Activities

3. Lift up the first flap and leave it uncut. Do not cut the bottom flap either. Cut vertically up through the second, third, fourth, and fifth flaps twice to divide the flaps into thirds.

4. Write "Step Through" and the name of your state on the top flap. Leave the last page for an illustration and student's name.

5. Write a question from the unit on each flap. Lift the flap and write the answer to the question underneath. You will have a total of twelve questions and answers.

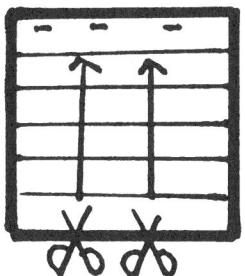
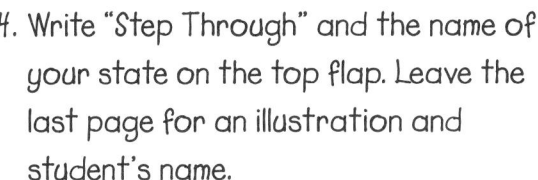
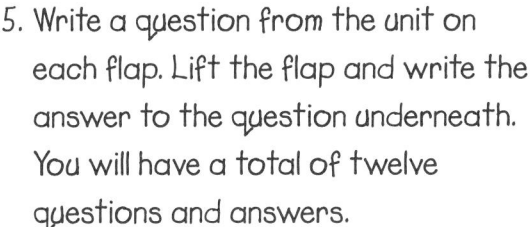

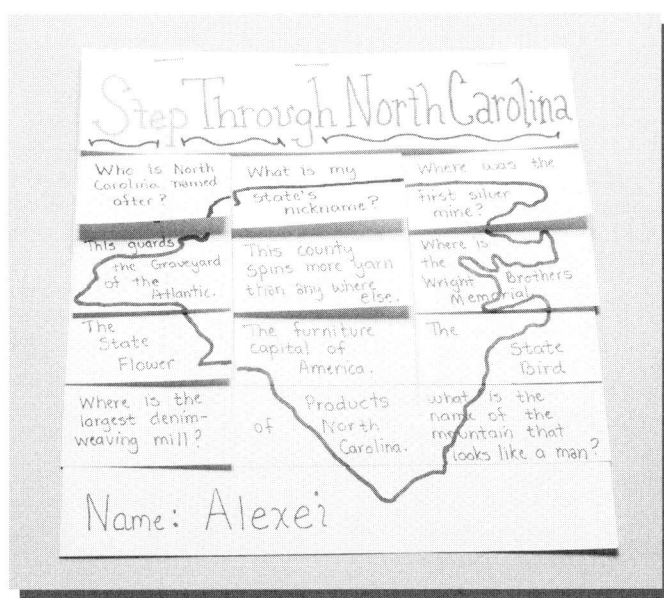

Hands-On Reading Activities

11

Snap-Shut Bag Book
Unit 4

Materials:
* 5 pint-size zip-top bags
* Blackline snapshots
* Colored duct tape
* Markers, colored pencils, or crayons
* Clear packaging tape

Social Studies Skills:
* Statehood
* Historic sites
* Early Life

Reading Skills:
* Fact and Opinion
* Inferences
* Sequencing

Instructions:
1. Lay two of the zip-top bags in front of you, one on top of the other, with the openings on the right. Cut a piece of packaging tape the length of the left side of the bags.
   IMPORTANT TIP: Do NOT make the tape longer than the bags.

2. Lay the tape half on and half off the top bag on the left side. Fold back the tape to bind the bottom bag to the top bag.

Illustrations:

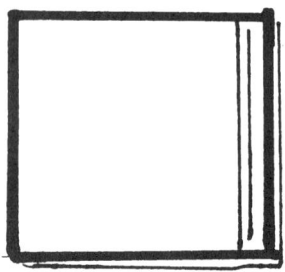

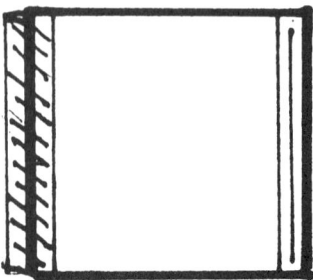

Hands-On Reading Activities

3. Place another bag on top of this set of bags, and repeat the taping process. Continue these steps until all five bags are bound together. Cover the taped edges with a piece of colored duct tape. Stick a small piece over the top and bottom of the taped edge to keep the pages from sliding.

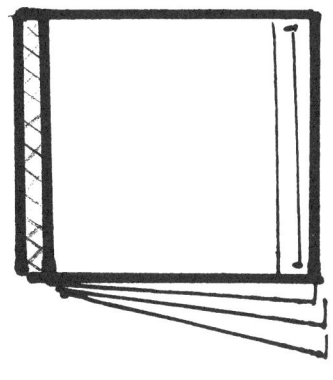

5. Using one snapshot blackline, make a cover with the name of the unit on it. Slip this into the top bag. Use more snapshot blacklines to illustrate and/or write about each lesson in the unit. Slip one snapshot into the back side of the cover bag, and put two more in each bag after that.

6. Students may decorate the last page and add their name and the date.

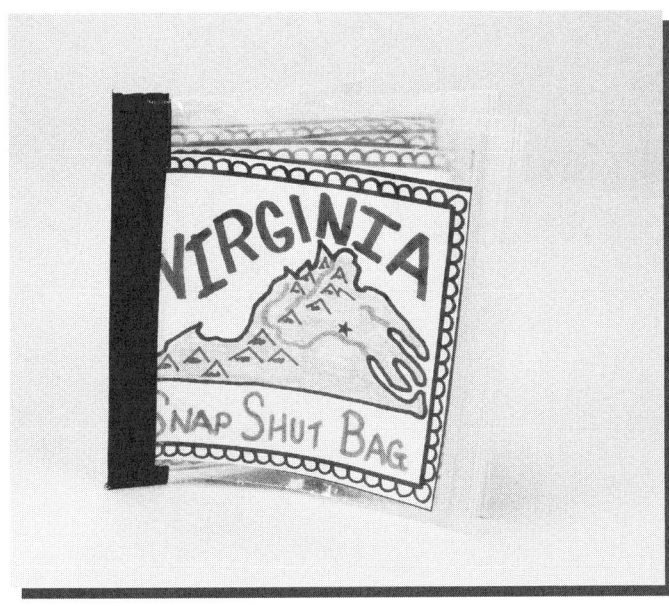

Hands-On Reading Activities

Design a Fact Hat
Unit 5

Materials:

*3 full-size sheets of newspaper

*2-inch-wide masking tape

*Scissors

*Construction paper (assorted)

*Velcro®

Social Studies Skills:

*Economics

*My State/World

*People Today

Reading Skills:

*Synonyms

*Questions

*Point of View

Instructions:

1. Students should work in groups of three.

   Student 1-head model
   Student 2-designer
   Student 3-tape-cutter

   Lay three open sheets of newspaper on Student 1's head.

2. Student 2 winds masking tape around Student 1's head three times.

Illustrations:

Hands-On Reading Activities

3. Student 2 folds up the edges of the newspaper to form a brim for the hat. Student 3 hands 1-inch pieces of tape to Student 2, who tapes the brim into place.

4. Hats can be spray painted for color.

5. Staple on a construction-paper hatband.

6. Write facts from the unit chapters on construction-paper rectangles and attach these to the hatband with Velcro™.

Hands-On Reading Activities

Fact Finder
Unit 6

Materials:

*One 8 1/2 x 11 sheet of paper
*Scissors
*Colored markers, crayons, colored pencils

Social Studies Skills:

*Local Government
*State Government
*Economics

Reading Skills:

*Categorizing
*Predict an Outcome
*Main Idea Facts

Instructions:

1. Fold the paper to form a square. Cut off and throw away the extra piece.

2. Open the square and fold it in half and in half again. Open the square.

3. Fold each corner in to the center.

4. Flip the square over. Again fold the corners to the center and press down.

Illustrations:

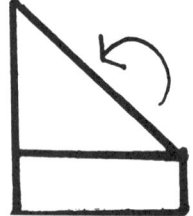
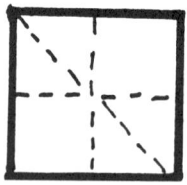
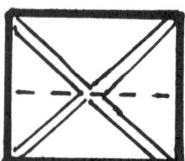

Hands-On Reading Activities

5. With points on top, fold this square in half and in half again. Open with the points facing up. Push the corners up until they meet.

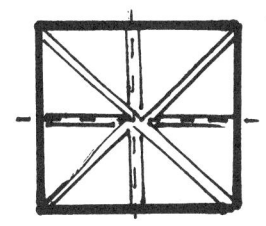

6. Pull the bottoms of the flaps out to form finger pockets. Put a color on the outside of each flap, a number on each inside section, and a question from the unit underneath each number. The answer goes in the space below the question.

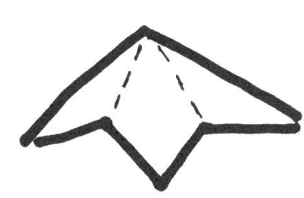

7. To play the game, one student holds the fact finder, and another student chooses a color. Then the "holder" moves the fact finder one time for each letter in the name of the selected color. The student chooses a number next, and the holder repeats the process. The student then selects another number, and the holder lifts the flap for the chosen number and reads the question. If the student answers correctly, he or she becomes the next holder.

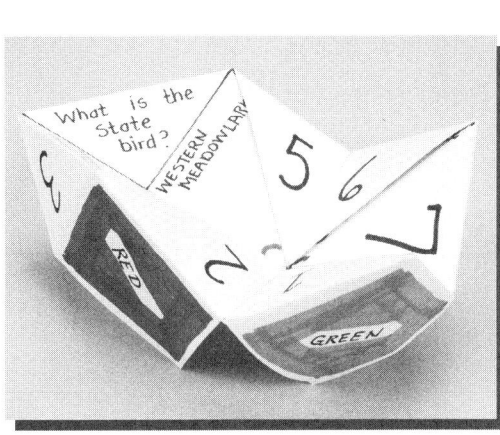

Hands-On Reading Activities

CD Case State Booklet

Snap-Shut Bag Book